CONTEMPORARY CRITICAL CRIMINOLOGY

The concept of critical criminology – that crime and the present-day processes of criminalization are rooted in the core structures of society – is of more relevance today than it has been at any other time.

Written by an internationally renowned scholar, *Contemporary Critical Criminology* introduces the most up-to-date empirical, theoretical, and political contributions made by critical criminologists around the world. In its exploration of this material, the book also challenges the erroneous but widely held notion that the critical criminological project is restricted to mechanically applying theories to substantive topics, or to simply calling for radical political, economic, cultural, and social transformations.

This book is an essential source of reference for both undergraduate and postgraduate students of Criminology, Criminal Theory, Social Policy, Research Methodology, and Penology.

Walter S. DeKeseredy is Professor of Criminology, Justice and Policy Studies at the Ontario University Institute of Technology, Canada. He is the author or co-author of 13 books on topics such as abuse of women, crime and poverty in public housing, and women in conflict with the law, and has also written over 70 scientific journal articles. Dr. DeKeseredy has received awards for his research from the American Society of Criminology's Division on Critical Criminology and Division on Women and Crime, as well as the Linda Saltzman Memorial Intimate Violence Researcher Award from the Institute on Violence, Abuse and Trauma.

KEY IDEAS IN CRIMINOLOGY

SERIES EDITOR: TIM NEWBURN is Professor of Criminology and Social Policy, Director of the Mannheim Centre for Criminology, London School of Economics and President of the British Society of Criminology. He has written and researched widely on issues of crime and justice.

Key Ideas in Criminology explores the major concepts, issues, debates, and controversies in criminology. The series aims to provide authoritative essays on central topics within the broader area of criminology. Each book adopts a strong individual "line," constituting original essays rather than literature surveys, and offers lively and agenda-setting treatments of their subject matter.

These books will appeal to students, teachers, and researchers in criminology, sociology, social policy, cultural studies, law, and political science.

Other titles in the series:

Penal Populism
John Pratt

Rehabilitation
Tony Ward and Shadd Maruna

Security
Lucia Zedner

Surveillance
Benjamin Goold

Feminist Criminology
Claire Renzetti

Public Criminology?
Ian Loader and Richard Sparks

Policing
Michael Kempa and Clifford Shearing

Genocidal Crimes
Alex Alvarez

Contemporary Critical Criminology
Walter S. DeKeseredy

CONTEMPORARY CRITICAL CRIMINOLOGY

Walter S. DeKeseredy

To Anne:
All the best.

LONDON AND NEW YORK

First published 2011
by Routledge
2 Park Square, Milton Park, Abingdon, Oxon OX14 4RN

Simultaneously published in the USA and Canada
by Routledge
270 Madison Avenue, New York, NY 10016

Routledge is an imprint of the Taylor & Francis Group, an informa business

Typeset in Sabon by Wearset Ltd, Boldon, Tyne and Wear
Printed and bound in Great Britain by TJ International Ltd, Padstow, Cornwall

British Library Cataloguing in Publication Data
A catalogue record for this book is available from the British Library

Library of Congress Cataloging-in-Publication Data
DeKeseredy, Walter S., 1959–
Contemporary critical criminology/by Walter S.
DeKeseredy.
p. cm.
Includes bibliographical references.
1. Critical criminology. 2. Criminology. I. Title.
HV6019.D45 2010
364–dc22   2010004664

ISBN13: 978-0-415-55667-5 (hbk)
ISBN13: 978-0-415-55666-8 (pbk)
ISBN13: 978-0-203-86923-9 (ebk)

Contents

PREFACE

In June of 1986, I would have never dreamed of writing this book. I was a second-year Ph.D. student with a keen interest in critical criminology, and I presented a paper titled "Marxist Criminology in Canada: Toward Linking Theory with Practice" at the Canadian Sociology and Anthropology conference in Winnipeg, Canada. I did not have a sophisticated understanding of critical criminology and thus did not expect my paper to be well received. However, things went worse than I anticipated. The discussant on my panel was a pioneer in the field and he sharply criticized my work in front of an audience of seasoned scholars for nearly 30 minutes. My self-esteem was shattered and I thought my career was over. I also vowed never to engage with critical criminology again. As is often said, "Never say never."

My supervisory committee helped me move forward and continue working on my dissertation. So, eager to keep up with new developments in my area of research, I attended the American Society of Criminology conference in Atlanta in November 1986 and went to sessions featuring prominent critical criminologists such as Meda Chesney-Lind, Kathleen Daly, Susan Caringella, Dorie Klein, Betsy Stanko, Russell and Rebecca Dobash, and Claire Renzetti. I was deeply moved by their passion, research, and critiques of mainstream research, theories, and policies. Their voices also started to rekindle my interest in critical criminology and they offered me alternative ways of understanding the social world.

Although these and other progressive scholars' presentations were in and of themselves important to me, what also brought me back to critical criminology was a long conversation I had with Kathleen Daly, Meda Chesney-Lind, Dorie Klein, and Betsy Stanko in a bar located in the conference hotel. They inspired me to pursue my inner desire to engage in feminist inquiry and other ways of thinking critically about crime. I would not be doing what I am doing today without their kindness, collegiality, and compassion. My dear friend and colleague Martin Schwartz also played a key role in returning me to critical criminology. I met Marty in 1987 and we have worked very closely together ever since.

There are actually quite a few good books on critical criminology, which is one of the key reasons I was somewhat reluctant to write this one. However, Routledge editor Gerhard Boomgaarden enthusiastically encouraged me to contribute a book on the topic to the *Key Ideas in Criminology* series edited by Tim Newburn. I am grateful for their support and hope that my project adds to the rapidly growing international body of critical criminological scholarship. Indeed, as I learned from working on this book, keeping up with the extant literature in the field constitutes a major ongoing challenge.

Contemporary Critical Criminology has several main objectives, one of which is to review my colleagues' recent empirical, theoretical, and political contributions. Another goal is to show that, contrary to what many conservative scholars claim, critical criminologists are heavily involved in theory construction and theory testing, and use a variety of research methods to gather qualitative and quantitative data. Critical criminologists also don't simply call for radical social, political, and economic change. Although this is one of their central goals, progressive scholars and activists also propose numerous short-term ways of chipping away at broader social forces that influence crime and buttress unjust laws and methods of social control. Hence, recent examples of such initiatives are discussed.

Chapter 1 offers readers a brief history and definition of critical criminology. Of course, an unknown number of readers will disagree with my historical account. Still, as Raymond Michalowski states in his 1996 story of critical criminology: "This is all to the good. I increasingly suspect that we can best arrive at useful truth by telling and hearing multiple versions of the same story" (Michalowski, 1996, p. 9).

Chapter 2 demonstrates that critical criminology has gone through a number of significant theoretical changes since its birth in the early 1970s. Special attention is paid to briefly reviewing and evaluating major new directions, such as cultural criminology, convict criminology, feminist theories, and recent variants of left realist thought. Undoubtedly, new perspectives will be offered by the time you finish reading this book.

Critical criminologists have done much empirical work over the past 40 years, and a key objective of Chapter 3 is to show that critical criminology is much more than a theoretical and/or political enterprise. Examples of recent research are presented, but the studies reviewed are not considered better than those not examined. Obviously, it is impossible to review all critical criminological empirical projects in one chapter or book.

What is to be done about crime, law, and social control? Chapter 4 shows that just because critical scholars call for major political, economic, social, and cultural transformations does not mean that they disregard short-term reforms. However, rather than repeat what has been said in previous critical texts, this chapter presents some new initiatives, such as using computer technology to protest government policies. It is necessary to create policies and practices that meet the unique needs of people in an ever-changing world, and the Internet is an effective means of facilitating social change.

Critical criminology is often criticized for being "gender-blind." True, early works, such as Taylor, Walton, and Young's (1973) *The New Criminology*, said nothing about women and the gendered nature of society; however, things have changed considerably since the publication of this seminal book. Thus, materials on women and gender are integrated into every chapter at relevant points. It isn't only gender issues that are fully integrated; race, class, *and* gender are treated as equally important and are brought up whenever they are relevant. Nevertheless, the bulk of the material on these factors are recent contributions, which is why this book is titled *Contemporary Critical Criminology*.

Acknowledgments

This book is the product of a collective effort. Again, it would not have been written without Gerhard Boomgaarden's kind invitation and support. Gerhard deeply cares about his authors and I count myself lucky to have had the pleasure of working closely with him. Series editor Tim Newburn also played a key role in bringing this book to fruition and I greatly respect his scholarly rigor and many important contributions to a social scientific understanding of some of the world's most compelling social problems. Routledge editorial assistant Jennifer Dodd became involved in this project shortly before it was completed and her patience and encouragement will always be remembered.

Others also deserve special recognition. Joseph F. Donnermeyer, David O. Friedrichs, Christopher W. Mullins, Stephen L. Muzzatti, Dawn Rothe, Martin D. Schwartz, and Phillip Shon took time away from their very busy schedules to carefully read drafts of each chapter despite having many responsibilities (including writing their own books, articles, etc.). I am thankful for their friendship, and they are scholars in the true spirit of the word. Their comments made this book better than it otherwise would have been.

Over the years I have greatly benefited from the comments, criticisms, lessons, emotional support, and influences of these progressive friends and colleagues: Bernie Auchter, Karen Bachar, Gregg Barak, Raquel Kennedy Bergen, Helene Berman, Henry Brownstein, Susan Caringella, Meda Chesney-Lind, Taylor Churchill, Kimberly J. Cook, Francis T. Cullen, Elliott Currie, Kathleen Daly, Molly Dragiewicz, Desmond Ellis, Jeff Ferrell, Bonnie Fisher, Alberto Godenzi, Judith Grant, Ronald Hinch, David Kauzlarich, Dorie Klein, Julian Lo, Michael J. Lynch, Brian D. MacLean, James W. Messerschmidt, Raymond

1

CRITICAL CRIMINOLOGY

DEFINITION AND BRIEF HISTORY

> [P]ossessive individualism is crumbling under its own weight of numbers. Despite building more and more prisons, despite incarcerating or seeking to control (by electronic or social engineering) human activity, the centre does not hold, mere anarchy holds sway. For at the heart of society there remains the "genetic" code of private property. It is inconceivable that criminology wedded to the "cure" rather than the causes of crime can in any way help permanently to resolve the crime problem. This would be the medical equivalent of accepting that an expanding tobacco industry and growing cancers are inevitable.
>
> (Walton, 1998, p. 3)

In the current era, much, if not all, of the world was (and probably still is) experiencing numerous economic, social, and political crises. For example, 400,000 jobs were lost in Canada since the fall of 2008, and in September 2009 Diane Finley, federal Human Resources Minister, argued strongly against cutting the minimum work requirements to qualify for employment insurance (Whittington, 2009a).[1] The summer of 2009 was, to say the least, also depressing for many Canadian youths aged 18–24. Approximately one out of every four Canadians in this age group was unemployed; with a sizeable portion unable to pay university or college tuition in the fall (Galt, 2009). Simultaneously, the youth unemployment rate in the United States hit a record high of 18.5 percent (Bureau of Labor Statistics, 2009).

The North American unemployment situation is not likely to improve in the near future. As Canadian Parliamentary Budget Officer Kevin Page noted in July 2009, Canada could lose 1.2 million jobs in 2009 and 2010. He also predicted that the federal budget deficit over five years will reach C$155.9 billion (Whittington, 2009b). With such high rates of unemployment comes chronic poverty, which in turn spawns more predatory violent street crimes, illegal drug use and dealing, and a myriad of other injurious symptoms of "turbo-charged capitalism" in poor communities (DeKeseredy, Alvi, Schwartz, and Tomaszewski, 2003; Luttwak, 1995).

As paid work in advanced capitalist countries and elsewhere rapidly disappears, we still witness many highly injurious effects of patriarchal gender relations. For instance, the World Health Organization conducted a multi-country study of the health effects of domestic violence. Over 24,000 women who resided in urban and rural parts of 10 countries were interviewed: the research team discovered that the percentage of women who were ever physically or sexually assaulted (or both) by an intimate partner ranged from 15 percent to 71 percent, with most research sites ranging between 29 percent and 62 percent (Garcia-Moreno, Jansen, Ellsberg, Heise, and Watts, 2005).

Another major international study – the International Violence Against Women Survey (IVAWS) – conducted interviews with 23,000 women in 11 countries. The percentage of women who revealed at least one incident of physical or sexual violence by any man since the age of 16 ranged from 20 percent in Hong Kong to between 50 percent and 60 percent in Australia, Costa Rica, the Czech Republic, Denmark, and Mozambique. In most countries examined, rates of victimization were above 35 percent (Johnson, Ollus, and Nevala, 2008). Consider, too, that in Australia, Canada, Israel, South Africa, and the United States, 40–70 percent of female homicide victims were murdered by their current or former partners (DeKeseredy, in press a; Krug, Dahlberg, and Mercy *et al.*, 2002). Another frightening fact is that 14 girls and women are killed each day in Mexico (Mujica and Ayala, 2008). Of course, male violence against female intimates takes many other shapes and forms, such as honor killings, dowry-related violence, and acid burning (Sev'er, 2008; Silvestri and Crowther-Dowey, 2008; Watts and Zimmerman, 2002). Annually, approximately 5,000 women and girls lose their lives to honor killings around the world (Proudfoot, 2009).

Racism, in its many shapes and forms, is also very much alive and well throughout the world despite major legislative changes and the ongoing efforts of human-rights groups and activists. In the United States, for example, 23 percent of Native Americans live below the poverty line, compared to 12 percent of the general population. To make matters worse, the poverty rate on US Native reservations is over 50 percent (Housing Assistance Council, 2002; Perry, 2009a). And, as Turpin-Petrosino (2009, p. 21) reminds us, in the United States, "[s]ome of the most notorious hate crimes ever committed have targeted blacks." Black US males are also incarcerated at a per capita rate six times higher than their white counterparts. Further, about 11 percent of black men aged 30–34 are incarcerated (Human Rights Watch, 2008).

What is to be done about unemployment, violence against women, racism, and a host of other problems that plague countries characterized by structured social inequality? Guided by the views of the late University of Chicago economist Milton Friedman (1962),[2] many people on the right, like former US President George W. Bush, contend that the solutions to the world's problems are found in the following trinity: the elimination of the public sector; total corporate liberation; and skeletal social spending (N. Klein, 2007). Ironically, many conservatives do not seem to have a problem spending taxpayers' money on building more prisons and incarcerating more people. For example, California is home to the largest prison system in the United States, and this state's corrections budget was $2.1 billion annually at the end of the 1980s. In 2008–2009, California's corrections budget rose to $10.1 billion (Legislative Analyst's Office, 2010).

Correction facilities now constitute a major industry in the United States and United Kingdom. There is a rapid growth in private prisons and many stock analysts are encouraging their clients to invest in major companies operating facilities such as the GEO Group, formally known as Wackenhut Securities (Reiman and Leighton, 2010). Private companies claim to run prisons at 10–20 percent lower cost than US state governments, but Austin and Coventry's (2001) study – sponsored by the National Institute of Justice – found it was only 1 percent.

If there is a military–industrial complex that profits from the wars in Iraq and Afghanistan, there is also a "prison–industrial complex" that gains from crime at the taxpayers' expense (Schlosser, 1998). Thus, it is more than fair to assume that big business has a vested interest in ensuring that crime rates stay high and that the incarceration rate – like profits – constantly grows (Selman and Leighton, 2010). As Reiman and Leighton (2010) note:

> *[T]he rich get richer* BECAUSE *the poor get prison!* Consider that in 2007, the top wage earner at CCA made $2.8 million and his counterpart at the Geo Group made $3.8 million, including stock options and all bonuses; the annual retainer for serving on the Board of Directors of either company is $50,000 (plus several thousand dollars for each meeting that Board members attend), which is close to the median household income of the United States in 2007.
>
> (p. 177; emphasis in original)

Not all conservatives view prisons or other elements of the criminal justice system as the primary cures for crime. One recent example is Canadian psychologist Donald Dutton (2006), who prefers "treating" wife-beaters to mandatory arrest policies. Like prisons, psychotherapy, counseling, psychosurgery, or any of a number of other techniques designed to help offenders identify and deal with their problems contribute little, if anything, to lowering crime rates. Such strategies suffer from what Elliott Currie (1985) calls the "fallacy of autonomy." The idea of autonomy is that people act on their own, without the influence of others. The implication of theories that inform individual treatment is that peer groups and broader social forces have little impact on people's behaviors, attitudes, norms, and values (DeKeseredy and Schwartz, 1996). Those who break the law are seen as living in a "world strangely devoid of social or economic consequences, even of history" (Currie, 1985, p. 215).

This is true of some offenders. However, most violent street crimes, especially those committed by youths, are committed in groups (Warr, 2002). This is why incarcerating or "treating" several gang members does nothing to lower the rate of violent crime in the United States (Currie, 2008a). You can lock people up or make them undergo therapy, but such measures do not eliminate the social, psychological, or interpersonal forces that influence people to harm others. For every gang member you take off the street, others will replace him or her.

If people's peers motivate them to commit violent acts, the same can be said about broader structural forces. It is, for example, not surprising that the violent crime rate in the United States is higher than that of most other highly industrialized societies (Currie, 2008a; Van Dijk, 2008). It is well known that the United States is a nation characterized by gross economic inequality, poverty, high infant mortality rates, homelessness, and inadequate social support services (for example, unemployment insurance and health care) (Schwartz and DeKeseredy, 2008). High rates of violent acts are major symptoms of these problems (DeKeseredy *et al.*, 2003), and these crimes are committed mainly by groups of "underclass" people, sometimes referred to as "the truly disadvantaged" (Blau and Blau, 1982; Wilson, 1987). In fact, social and economic inequality – not personality or biological factors – are the most powerful predictors of most violent crimes (DeKeseredy, in press a).

Are there useful and meaningful alternatives to conventional wisdom about crime and its control? In other words, is there a progressive school of thought that sees crime as something other than a property of the individual and that views broader social, political, and economic change as the best solution to crimes in the streets, suites, and domestic/intimate settings? Anyone familiar with social scientific empirical, theoretical, and policy work would quickly point out that sociologists provide different ways of thinking about crime, deviance, and social control. Indeed, they do and some of them have had an important impact on public policy over the past 50 years. Consider strain theorists Richard Cloward and Lloyd Ohlin (1960). Their differential opportunity theory of delinquent subcultures was extremely important in the history of criminological and deviance theory, in that perhaps no other theory was responsible for generating so much government funding in the United States (DeKeseredy, Ellis, and Alvi, 2005). The logic was that if gang membership was a function of a lack of legitimate opportunity structures for youths, then the solution was to increase these opportunities. Under President Kennedy, and especially under President Johnson with his "War on Poverty" in the 1960s, a wide variety of programs were instituted to deal with educational deficiencies and job training. Unfortunately, under what Curran and Renzetti (2001) call the late President Reagan's "War on the Poor" in the 1980s, those programs not earlier eliminated by President Nixon were killed off, and today, there is still considerable resistance in the United States to implementing policies guided by Cloward and Ohlin, and others with similar perspectives on social problems.

Most sociologists who study crime, though, are what some criminologists would refer to as "liberal progressives." In other words, they: accept official definitions of crime (e.g., legal definitions); ignore concepts and theories offered by Marxist, feminist, critical race, and other "radical" scholars; call for fine-tuning state institutions' responses to social problems (e.g., expand the role of the welfare state); pay little – if any – attention to the role of broader social forces, and primarily use quantitative methods to collect and analyze crime and criminal justice data (Ratner, 1985).

Metaphorically speaking, critical criminologists, on the other hand, throw bricks through establishment or mainstream criminology's windows (Young, 1998). "[R]esolutely sociological in orientation" (Carrington and Hogg, 2008, p. 5), critical criminologists oppose official definitions of crime, official statistics (e.g., police arrest data), and positivism, but are for social justice, human rights, and the like (Stubbs, 2008). Positivism assumes that human behavior is determined and can be measured (Curran and Renzetti, 2001). Moreover, within the discipline of criminology, there is "an enduring commitment to measurement" (Hagan, 1985, p. 78).

The primary objective of this book is to provide readers with a brief scholarly overview of critical criminology, which has undergone many changes since its birth roughly 40 years ago. It is defining critical criminology that I turn to next.

DEFINITION OF CRITICAL CRIMINOLOGY

Although the term has been around since the early 1970s, many criminologists are still not exactly sure what the words *critical criminology* mean (DeKeseredy and Perry, 2006a). This applies not only to people who do not consider themselves critical criminologists, but also to people who actually feel that they are part of the tradition. Although various definitions have been proposed, there is no widely accepted precise formulation (Stubbs, 2008). However, for the purpose of this book, I offer a modified version of Jock Young's (1988) definition of radical criminology. Here, critical criminology is defined as a perspective that views the major sources of crime as the unequal class, race/ethnic, and gender relations that control our society. Certainly, as Schwartz and Hatty (2003) observe, "there are many types of critical criminology as there are writers and teachers in the area" (p. ix), and this book is specifically crafted to reflect this diversity.

Stubbs (2008), Carrington and Hogg (2008), Michalowski (1996), and others (e.g., DeKeseredy and Perry, 2006a) repeatedly note, there is no single critical criminology. Rather, there are critical criminologies that have different origins, use different methods, and that have diverse political beliefs. Nevertheless, as Friedrichs (2009) observes, "The unequal distribution of power or of material resources within contemporary societies provides a unifying point of departure for all strains of critical criminology" (p. 210). Another common feature all critical criminologists share is the rejection of solutions to crime measures such as "zero-tolerance" policing (e.g., criminalizing incivilities like panhandling), three-strikes sentencing, private prisons, coercive counseling therapy, and so on. Instead, critical criminologists regard major structural and cultural changes within society as essential steps to reduce crime and promote social justice.

Still, just because critical criminologists call for major economic, political, and cultural transformations does not mean that they totally disregard criminal justice reform, an issue of paramount concern to conservative scholars, politicians, journalists, and members of the general public. After all, every society requires a mixture of formal and informal means of social control (Michalowski, 1985). Still, the types of criminal justice reform called for do not include more punitive initiatives or hurtful forms of psychological treatment, such as the cruel electroshock "treatment" carried out in the 1950s in Montreal by Dr. Ewen Cameron at McGill University's Allan Memorial Institute. Funded by the Central Intelligence Agency (CIA), Cameron's unethical medical experiments also involved isolating people for weeks, keeping them asleep for lengthy periods of time, and the administration of "drug cocktails," including LSD and PCP. At least nine people who went to Cameron seeking relief from minor psychiatric problems (e.g., depression) ended up being used "without their knowledge and permission, as human guinea pigs to satisfy the CIA's thirst for information about how to control the human mind" (N. Klein, 2007, p. 31).

Some things don't change. As Naomi Klein (2007) vividly describes in her riveting book, *The Shock Doctrine: The Rise of Disaster Capitalism*, Cameron played a major role in creating recent US government torture techniques, such as those recently applied to inmates at Guantanamo. She notes:

> Indeed, in the testimonies, reports and photographs that have come out of Guantanamo, it is as if the Allan Memorial Institute of the 1950s had been transported to Cuba. When first detained, prisoners are put into intense sensory deprivation, with hoods, blackout goggles and heavy headphones to block out all sound. They are left in isolation cells for months, taken out only to have their senses bombarded with barking dogs, strobe light and endless tape loops of babies crying, music blaring and cats meowing.
>
> (p. 51)

Critical criminologists define the actions of Cameron and those who tortured inmates at Guantanamo as crimes. In addition, they call for progressive short-term policies that target the major social, political, cultural, and economic forces that propel people into crime, such as poverty, sexism, and deindustrialization. Of course, critical criminologists are not the only ones who call for such strategies. Recall that some initiatives informed by Cloward and Ohlin (1960), as well as other strain theorists (e.g., Merton, 1938), are also designed to maximize people's educational and employment opportunities. Consider that one new direction in critical criminology – left realism – is well known in the field for advancing strategies such as a higher minimum wage and state-sponsored, affordable, and quality health care (DeKeseredy, Alvi, and Schwartz, 2006).

Critical criminology has gone through many significant changes since its inception and it will continue to evolve because its proponents advance progress (DeKeseredy and Perry, 2006b). Still, just because something is "old" does not mean that it is no longer valuable. For example, nearly 15 years ago, in the introduction to their anthology, *Thinking Critically about Crime*, Brian MacLean and Dragan Milovanovic (1997a, p. 15) observed that, "far from being 'hegemonic,' and far from being monolithic in its thinking, critical criminology is a discipline characterized by a rich theoretical diversity." Trees with many branches have one trunk. Similarly, while there are different ways of thinking critically about crime, critical criminology has some important common characteristics, such as those described previously. In addition, critical criminologists disavow all criminologists as "neutral scientific experts" (Stubbs, 2008, p. 7). They also have no problem being labeled *political*. After all, as the famous French philosopher Jean Paul Sartre (1964) put it, "all writing is political" (p. 29), and critical criminologists want their work to help reduce much pain and suffering. Moreover, like many other contemporary social scientists, critical criminologists contend that no scientific method, theory, or policy is value free (DeKeseredy and Dragiewicz, 2007).

In one of the most widely read and cited social scientific articles in the world, Howard Becker (1967) asks sociologists, "Whose side are we on?" By now, most, if not all, readers have figured out that critical criminologists are on the side of the socially and economically excluded. Included in this group of "outsiders" (Becker, 1973) are victims of human-rights violations, those who lost jobs because corporations like General Motors moved operations to developing nations, people lacking adequate social services (e.g., health care and child care), and the targets of state terrorism, such as those imprisoned at Guantanamo (Schwendinger and Schwendinger, 1975; Tepperman, 2010). Critical criminologists want to broaden the definition of crime to include the harms listed above, as well as racism, sexism, imperialism, and corporate wrongdoings (Elias, 1986; Reiman and Leighton, 2010).

Kubrin, Stucky, and Krohn (2009) claim that the critical criminological "literature is characterized by too many ideas and not enough systematic research and that most empirical studies are illustrative of, but do not actually *test* the theory" (p. 239; emphasis in original). Nothing could be further from the truth. Another thing that brings critical criminologists together is years of in-depth research using a variety of methods, including ethnography, biography, narrative, deconstruction, and other qualitative methods (Lynch, Michalowski, and Groves, 2000). Phillipe Bourgois' (1995) study is an excellent example of pathbreaking critical criminological research that involved the collection of in-depth ethnographic data derived from five years spent in East Harlem (also referred to as El Barrio) observing, tape recording, and photographing various components of the lives of roughly 24 Puerto Rican crack dealers.

In some ways, Bourgois' work resembles that of Oscar Lewis' mid-1960s research (see his 1966 bestselling book, *La Vida*). For example, both scholars are anthropologists and both have done ethnographic research in El Barrio. However, they offer fundamentally different interpretations of the sources of poverty there and the myriad of social problems related to this highly injurious symptom of structured social inequality. Based on life-history data provided by one extended Puerto Rican family, Lewis' offering is the culture-of-poverty theory, which contends that middle-class and lower-class values are distinct. Instead of addressing how broader political, economic, and cultural forces are related to social and economic exclusion, he and more contemporary culture-of-poverty theorists argue that the poor are poor because, unlike middle-class people, they lack the moral fiber and discipline to get an education, to get jobs, defer gratification, and so on.

On the other hand, Bourgois' account asserts that macro-level factors such as the following have fueled the emergence of

Puerto Rican drug-dealing gangs in El Barrio: the rapid expansion of the finance, insurance, and real estate (FIRE) sector in New York City; the North American Free Trade Agreement (NAFTA); transnational corporations moving operations to make use of cheap labor; the implementation of high technology in the workplace; and the shift from a manufacturing to a service-based economy. Bourgois also contends that these ghetto-based criminal subcultures are not distinct from the wider or mainstream US culture. On the contrary, they are a core element of US culture and are actively involved in the pursuit of the "American Dream" and the respect garnered from it.

Bourgois argues:

> Like most other people in the United States, drug dealers and street criminals are scrambling to obtain their piece of the pie as fast as possible. In fact, in their pursuit of success they are even following the minute details of the classical Yankee model for upward mobility. They are aggressively pursuing careers as private entrepreneurs; they take risks, work hard, and pray for good luck. They are the ultimate rugged individualists braving an unpredictable frontier where fortune, fame, and destruction are all around the corner, where the enemy is ruthlessly hunted down and shot.
>
> (Bourgois, 1995, p. 326)

Although he does not specifically identify himself as an anomie, a subcultural, or as a left realist theorist, Bourgois' perspective is obviously heavily informed by the work of Albert Cohen (1955), Robert K. Merton (1938), Steven Messner and Richard Rosenfeld (2006), and Jock Young (1999). Note that left realists assert that inner-city people who lack legitimate means of solving the problem of relative deprivation come into contact with other frustrated disenfranchised people and form subcultures, which in turn encourage and legitimate criminal behaviors (Lea and Young, 1984). As Bourgois discovered, receiving respect from peers is highly valued among El Barrio males who are denied status in mainstream, middle-class society. Moreover, his work helps sensitize readers to how critical criminologists borrow some concepts and methods from mainstream scholars to help demonstrate how various types of inequality influence people to commit crime and to the ways in which these social forces affect societal reactions to crime and incivilities (DeKeseredy, in press b).

There is another problem with Kubrin *et al.*'s (2009) characterization of critical criminology. Critical criminology is not devoid of theory testing, and contrary to what many mainstream criminologists assert, there are groups of critical criminologists who use quantitative methods. For example, using nationwide representative sample survey data on woman abuse in university/college dating gathered in Canada, Martin D. Schwartz and I tested hypotheses derived from feminist theories, male-peer-support theory, and routine-activities theory (DeKeseredy and Schwartz, 1998; Schwartz and DeKeseredy, 1997). Moreover, as a "card carrying" critical criminologist, it was not until the early part of this decade that I conducted a purely qualitative study (see DeKeseredy and Schwartz, 2009).

DeKeseredy *et al.* (2003) provide another reason why people unfamiliar with critical criminological research should not assume that all critical scholars only use qualitative methods. Heavily informed by Jock Young's (1999) theoretical work on social and economic exclusion, feminist perspectives on woman abuse, and other progressive schools of thought, their project involved administering a victimization survey, in-depth interviews with public housing residents, and the analyses of available Canadian census tract and enumeration data.

There is much empirical diversity found in critical criminological literature, which reflects the view that research methods are tools that can be used in a variety of ways to achieve a variety of goals. Consider something as simple as a shovel. It can be used to build a shelter for the homeless and a private prison that houses and punishes poor victims of the US government's "war on drugs." Obviously, critical criminologists prefer using a shovel to build a shelter and use research methods to reveal how broader social forces contribute to crime and draconian means of social control (DeKeseredy and Perry, 2006a).

Prior to the mid-1980s, the objects of study for critical criminologists were mainly the ruling elite, corporate and white-collar criminals, law-breaking government officials, and the people who make the decisions on what is to be criminalized and what is not (DeKeseredy and Schwartz, 1996). Today, as described in more detail in Chapter 3, critical criminology involves the study of crime from all directions, including in the "suites," on the streets, and in domestic/household settings.

Since critical criminologists use a variety of empirical techniques and study a wide range of topics, it could easily be argued that many of these progressive scholars are interested in the same questions as other criminologists, such as: Why do people deal drugs or commit predatory street crimes? The most important difference is that they are not likely to look at flaws in the makeup of individuals, or study the "inherent" pathologies of particular groups, but rather they focus on the flaws in the makeup of a society that breeds, creates, and sustains such people (DeKeseredy and Perry, 2006a).

Theoretical and empirical work done by critical criminologists often involves "mixing and matching" (Schwartz and Hatty, 2003). In addition to borrowing concepts from mainstream theories, critical criminologists "create for themselves identities that cross over several subfields" of progressive thought and research (p. x), and these identities change according to the topics studied. For example, Martin Schwartz and I draw from left realism to explain inner-city predatory street crime and are guided by feminist and male-peer-support theories in our work on woman abuse. Rather than strictly adhere to one position, contemporary critical criminologists "are able to balance more than one belief at the same time" and often find that "an amalgam of two or more theories satisfies them intellectually" (Schwartz and Hatty, 2003, p. x).

In sum, then, the answer to the question "What do critical criminologists do?" is that they do many different empirical, theoretical, and political things. Still, as Elliott Currie (2008b) states in his brief commentary on the chapters included in Carrington and Hogg's (2008, p. vii) *Critical Criminology: Issues, Debates, Challenges*:

> There is no party line here; the contributors don't all speak with the same voice, but what links their diverse perspectives is a willingness to apply a critical lens not only to the work of their more conventional counterparts in the discipline but their own as well.

This can be said of all critical criminologists.

Critical criminology is definitely an intellectual movement (Michalowski, 1996), but it is much more than an academic enterprise. Included among critical criminology's diverse voices are people inside and outside the academy who devote the bulk or part of their energy and time to the progressive struggle for social change. For instance, in 2002, Lisa Simpson and two other plaintiffs filed a lawsuit against the University of Colorado. During a recruiting weekend, football players and recruits sexually assaulted them. In their lawsuit, the plaintiffs argued that there were previous assaults by players, the university was aware of these prior attacks, and that the university violated Title IX of the Education Amendments of 1972 by not acting to prevent further sexual assaults (Fleury-Steiner and Miller, 2008). This law states: "No person in the US shall, on the basis of sex, be excluded from participation in, be denied the benefits of, or be subjected to discrimination under any education program or activity receiving federal assistance" (US Department of Labor, 2009).

In 2005 a male judge dismissed the lawsuit. Needless to say, his decision was met with a giant outcry, especially among the feminist community, including members of the American Society of Criminology's Division on Women and Crime (DWC). Based at the University of Colorado at Boulder, feminist criminologist Joanne Belknap was among several people who helped the rape victims and she confronted and challenged the university's administration. Together with two colleagues, Belknap also created a consensual-sex training program for the University of Colorado's football team. Similar to many other women who challenge the patriarchal status quo, she experienced some of the vicious tactics of the anti-feminist backlash, such as threatening phone calls (Belknap, 2005; Fleury-Steiner and Miller, 2008).[3]

In honor of her activism, Belknap received the DWC's CoraMae Richey Mann "Inconvenient Woman of the Year" award, which "recognizes the scholar/activist who has participated in publicly promoting the ideals of gender equality and women's rights throughout society, particularly as it related to gender and crime issues." Like Belknap, Brian MacLean is another award-winning critical criminologist who helped stimulate social change. With two colleagues (Basran, Gill, and MacLean, 1995), he conducted a local Canadian survey of corporate violence against Punjabi farm-workers and their children. This study influenced Kwantlen University College and the British Columbia government to provide suitable and affordable child care for Punjabi farm-workers, and it is one of several empirically informed realistic solutions to unequal social conditions (Devine and Wright, 1993).

Over the past 30 years, critical criminology, as a discipline, has influenced many international organizations that struggle for social justice, including the Sentencing Project in the United States and Penal Reform International in England (Currie, 2008b). Critical criminologists are also members of such progressive organizations. For example, I serve on the Ohio Domestic Violence Network's advisory board and the California Coalition Against Sexual Assault's campus advisory board.

Nearly 30 years ago, critical criminology became institutionalized and established (Cohen, 1981). It is still this way today. As will be described in the next section of this chapter, we are witnessing what Jock Young (2008) observes as "the flourishing of critical criminology" (p. 259). However, even though critical criminologists have conducted pathbreaking studies, developed major theories, and proposed innovative ways of curbing crimes from all directions, many US criminologists, universities, politicians, criminal justice officials, members of the US general population, and even some textbook publishers are not receptive to their intellectual and political contributions. This is, of course, because they challenge the political, economic, and cultural status quo. To this day, many American critical criminologists experience hostility, academic isolation, and marginalization.

CRITICAL CRIMINOLOGY: A BRIEF HISTORY[4]

Critical criminology has its roots in what was once called *radical* criminology or *Marxist* criminology. Karl Marx himself said very little about crime (Schwartz and Hatty, 2003), but many critical criminologists, especially those who produced theories of crime and its control in the 1970s and early 1980s (e.g., Chambliss, 1975; Smandych, 1985; Spitzer, 1975), relied on Marxist analyses of capitalist society, and Taylor, Walton and Young's (1973) book, *The New Criminology: For a Social Theory of Deviance*, was especially important in the development of Marxist criminology (Matthews, 2003). Today, only a few critical criminologists identify themselves as Marxists, but the majority of them are concerned with class and how capitalism shapes crime, law, and social control (Schwartz and Hatty, 2003). Given the economic data presented at the start of this chapter and other symptoms of a global economic crisis, some critical criminologists correctly point out that "Marxism remains as relevant as ever for analyzing crime, criminal justice and the role of the state" (Russell, 2002, p. 113). For example, in the United States, Canada, and other capitalist countries, it is still primarily the socially and economically excluded who are incarcerated (De Giorgi, 2008; Wacquant, 2009). And, during this current period of staggering unemployment, like the "U.S. carceral archipelago," prisons around the world "swallow the growing number of people who do not compete on the regular labor market" (Hornqvist, 2008, p. 19). Of course, not everyone is equally likely to be a victim of violent crime, with those at the bottom of the socioeconomic ladder being at the highest risk (Currie, 2008a). For these and other reasons, then, critical criminologists are, to various extents, compelled to turn to Marx, "not because he is infallible, but because he is inescapable" (Heilbroner, 1980, p. 15).

Today, you will find critical criminologists around the world. However, the United States and the United Kingdom are the birthplaces of contemporary critical criminological thought (Sparks, 1980). Nevertheless, they have dissimilar academic histories. Although in the late 1960s and early 1970s academic sociologists were radicalized into the New Left in both the United Kingdom and the United States, the next steps were very different. In the United States, radicals rarely gained control over an entire department, and where they did – such as at the University of California (UC) at Berkeley – the result was more likely the disbanding of the department than the establishment of a beachhead of progressive theory, research, and praxis

(DeKeseredy and Schwartz, 1991a; Schwendinger, Schwendinger, and Lynch, 2008). Although isolated radicals have often been tolerated if they did not cause much trouble, radical criminologists and critical legal studies scholars have been heavily victimized by "academic McCarthyism" (Friedrichs, 1989). For example, the author of the widely read and cited 1969 book, *The Child Savers*, progressive criminologist Anthony Platt, was denied tenure at the UC at Berkeley in 1974 despite meeting the criteria of good teaching and excellent scholarship. At that time, the regents of the UC were conservative elites with major connections to the military–industrial complex, and they had the power to veto tenure recommendations (Schwendinger *et al.*, 2008). The UC at Berkeley chancellor was quoted as saying Platt was an "orthodox Marxist" and "biased in his teaching" (cited in Leonard, 1974, p. 1).

Fueled by extraordinary funding from the Law Enforcement Assistance Administration of the US Department of Justice for tuition scholarships for law-enforcement personnel, the main drive in US academic life was to found departments of criminal justice. With the majority of the students in these programs often either in-service or pre-service law enforcement, the major subject matter taught was commonly administrative criminology[5] and technical law enforcement. To staff hundreds of departments starting almost simultaneously, many schools hired line personnel from police and corrections agencies with limited training in academic criminology. In later years, these faculty duplicated themselves by requiring line experience in law enforcement for new faculty (DeKeseredy and Schwartz, 1991a).

As an obvious result, the curriculum focused on conservative "law and order" criminology and technical law enforcement. Students were primarily taught that crime is a property of the individual (the biological/psychological orientation), and that the most effective ways of dealing with criminals were to "police 'em, jail 'em [and maybe even] kill 'em" (Barak, 1986, p. 201). Although, to be sure, many radicals still taught courses in criminology or the sociology of deviant behavior, these courses were often marginalized to the edges of the discipline or only taught in sociology departments as electives for sociology majors. At the same time, enormous sums of money were available to criminologists doing research in administrative criminology, particularly studies designed to improve efficiency in criminal justice system operations (DeKeseredy and Schwartz, 1996).

Today, many US textbooks also marginalize critical criminologists. For example, most of the major criminology texts published each year in the United States purport to present a balanced view of the many conflicting theories within criminology. In fact, virtually none do, and perhaps this is an impossible goal to achieve. However, one area that is consistently given poor treatment is critical criminology. Some texts simply ignore this side of the field. Others give extensive coverage, perhaps an entire chapter, but limit themselves to ancient intellectual battles and detailed coverage of long-discredited leftist theories.

Even the prestigious American Society of Criminology (ASC) has a history of being unkind to critical criminologists. For instance, in 1979, some mainstream criminologists attacked radical criminologists in a special issue of *Criminology* (volume 16, Number 4, February 1979),[6] which is one of two official journals of the ASC. According to Schwendinger *et al.* (2008, p. 55): "This edition, devoted to radical criminology, was unprecedented. It was the first time any professional society had published a separate edition of its official journal aimed at discrediting an up-and-coming theoretical and policy perspective in the field." Nevertheless, events such as this have not stopped US critical criminologists in their tracks. Critical criminology is very much alive and well in the United States, as it is in the United Kingdom, Canada, and other countries.

The situation was quite different in the United Kingdom, where deviance courses were taught by sociology departments, and often by instructors affiliated with the National Deviance Conference. Radicals established "power bases" in various polytechnics (e.g., Middlesex, which was the "home" of left realists), universities, and colleges of education (Young, 1988). Since scholars such as those belonging to the left realist cohort were able to work in close proximity to each other, it is not surprising that united schools of thought were able to develop in the United Kingdom. One of the more recent of these is cultural criminology (Ferrell, Hayward, and Young, 2008), which is a major intellectual movement at the University of Kent in the United Kingdom – the home of the "cultural criminology team."

Another major difference is the effect that scholars have had outside the ivory towers of the academy. As with socialists and feminists generally, American radical criminologists have been marginalized on every level. Not only was there no national radical conference founded, but it was not until 1988 that radical criminologists felt strong enough to begin to work toward institutionalizing themselves as a division within the ASC (DeKeseredy and Schwartz, 1991a; Michalowski, 1996).

In the United Kingdom, critical criminological discourse has influenced Labour Party politics, especially at the local level in the 1980s, when Young (1988, p. 170) wrote:

> [a] new wave of young Labour politicians, many of them schooled in the New Left Orthodoxy of the sixties, were brought into power in the inner-city Labour strongholds. They – and in particular the police committee support units which they brought into being – became important political focuses for the ideas and concerns of radical criminology.

At the time Young made this statement, the connection between politicians and academics provided opportunities that were rarely available in the United States. Although, just as in the United States, the Home Office provided research grants only to administrative criminologists, the opportunity existed for radical criminologists to work through Labour-controlled local government offices. Further, there was no political group in the United States similar to the British Labour Party or the Canadian New Democratic Party, where socialists and other progressives were drawn to participate in mainstream political activities. To a small extent, the US Democratic Party adheres to some socialist principles, but that remains a slight variation with a dominant order committed to perpetuating and legitimating capitalist, patriarchal social relations (DeKeseredy, 2007; Miliband, 1969). Unfortunately, despite the popularity of President Barak Obama, we are already witnessing many Democrats adopting an approach Elliott Currie (1992) defined nearly 20 years ago as "progressive retreatism." This involves embracing parts of conservative policies to win elections. Furthermore, many critics now claim that the British Labour Party has lost its bearings and now resembles the US Republican Party.

Democratic Party meetings do not bring US radicals together to formulate agendas such as left realism, because their voices are likely to be ignored. Historically, the Democratic Party has not provided research opportunities for radical criminologists, even at the most local levels. However, during Bill Clinton's term as President of the United States, and since the passing of the 1994 Violence Against Women Act, a sizeable portion of research grants were given to feminist scholars by the US Justice Department to study key issues related to violence against women. For example, while I was based at Ohio University from 2000 to 2004, I received such a grant to conduct a qualitative study of separation/divorce sexual assault in rural Ohio – a project that was heavily informed by feminist theory and involved the use of feminist research methods (DeKeseredy and Schwartz, 2009).

In sum, political and academic forces have indirectly contributed to the development of a more united group of critical criminologists in the United Kingdom. Operating within more repressive political and academic contexts, US critical criminologists, until relatively recently, were forced to "go it alone." Their individual contributions, however, are important and warrant attention.

As stated previously, US criminology textbooks commonly devote little attention to critical scholarship beyond, say, a few brief statements on Taylor, Walton, and Young's (1973) *The New Criminology*. Further, most of these texts pay little, if any, attention to the critical work done in other countries such as Canada, Australia, Italy, Norway, Venezuela, and France, despite the fact that critical criminologists based there are engaged in pathbreaking scholarship, activism, and policy development. This cross-cultural or international approach is missing even in widely cited US critical texts, such as Lynch *et al.*'s (2000) *The New Primer in Radical Criminology*.

In Canada, where I live, while critical criminology may not be a core component of the broader Canadian criminology curriculum, critical criminologists are much more likely to hold tenured positions at prominent universities. This is due, in part, to the fact that progressive ways of studying and thinking about a host of social problems are highly respected in sociology departments. Further, Canada is witnessing a growth in new criminology programs, some of which include a large number of critical criminologists. For example, in the winter of 2010, approximately 11 critical criminologists were affiliated with the University of Ontario Institute of Technology's (UOIT) Faculty of Criminology, Justice, and Policy Studies. Moreover, *Critical Criminology*, the official journal of the ASC's Division on Critical Criminology (DCC) was also based at UOIT.

Critical criminology is an international enterprise and new information technologies make it easier for critical criminologists to exchange ideas with their peers based outside their respective countries and to develop collaborative projects. Nevertheless, much more needs to be done to develop a more inclusive critical criminology, one that routinely involves including scholarly work produced outside primarily English-speaking countries in books such as this one (DeKeseredy and Perry, 2006a). This will eventually happen because critical criminology is a never-ending and constantly evolving way of "doing criminology" (Lynch *et al.*, 2000).

Rural crime has ranked among the least studied social problems in criminology (DeKeseredy, Donnermeyer, Schwartz, Tunnell, and Hall, 2007). As Donnermeyer, Jobes, and Barclay (2006, p. 199) put it in their comprehensive review of rural crime research:

> If rural crime was considered at all, it was a convenient "ideal type" contrasted with the criminogenic conditions assumed to exist exclusively in urban locations. Rural crime was rarely examined, either comparatively with urban crime or a subject of investigation in its own right.

Critical criminology, too, is guilty of devoting selective inattention to rural issues (Donnermeyer and DeKeseredy, 2008). However, today there is a growth in critical criminological analyses of rural crime and societal reactions to it, such as the work of Hogg and Carrington (2006) in Australia, DeKeseredy and Schwartz's (2009) feminist research on separation/divorce sexual assault in rural Ohio, and UK scholars Chakraborti and Garland's (2004) contribution to a critical understanding of rural racism. Judith Grant's (2008) feminist analysis of Appalachian Ohio women's pathways from addiction to recovery is another important contribution to the field. Moreover, heavily influenced by Taylor *et al.*'s (1973) *New Criminology* and by research on "gendered violence and the architecture of rural life" (Hogg and Carrington, 2006, p. 171), Donnermeyer and DeKeseredy (2008) outline some key elements of a new or critical rural criminology that does not privilege class over gender.

Of course, the critical criminological project will always be incomplete, which is a blessing rather than a curse. Critical criminologists fully recognize that resisting change, or advancing standardization of theory, method, and policy "is the parent of stagnation" (Jacobs, 2004, p. 119; see also DeKeseredy and Perry, 2006a).

THE CURRENT STATE OF CRITICAL CRIMINOLOGY[7]

Twenty-five years after the publication of *The New Criminology*, two of its co-authors, Paul Walton and Jock Young (1988, p. vii) stated that:

> Radical criminology ... has since proliferated, developed and flourished. The various currents that form its past, whether Marxist, radical feminist or anarchist, continue in fierce dispute but have in common the notion that crime and the present day processes of criminalization are rooted in the core structures of society, whether its class nature, its patriarchal form or its inherent authoritarianism.

What they said then is true today. As is frequently pointed out, critical criminology is even stronger than when Walton and Young published their seminal anthology, *The New Criminology Revisited* (DeKeseredy and Perry, 2006a). For example, the ASC's DCC now has nearly 400 members, many of whom are based outside the United States and the United Kingdom. Again,